Stranger Than Fiction

EPIC FAILS

By Virginia Loh-Hagan

Disclaimer: This series focuses on the strangest of the strange. Have fun reading about strange people and things! But please do not try any of the antics in this book. Be safe and smart!

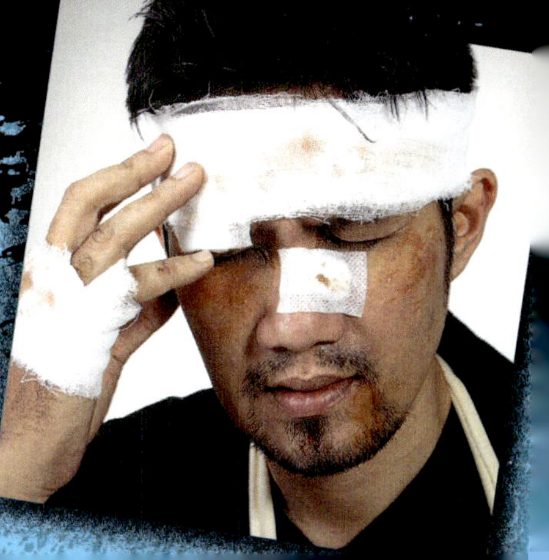

45th Parallel Press

Published in the United States of America by Cherry Lake Publishing
Ann Arbor, Michigan
www.cherrylakepublishing.com

Reading Adviser: Marla Conn MS, Ed., Literacy specialist, Read-Ability, Inc.
Book Designer: Melinda Millward

Photo Credits: © LukaszPanek/iStockphoto, cover, 12; © Pepsco Studio/Shutterstock.com, 1; © Lucian Coman/Shutterstock.com, 5, 30; © Jat306/Shutterstock.com, 6; © Alan Band/Fox Photos/Getty Images, 7; © pathdoc/Shutterstock.com, 8; © Andrey_Popov/Shutterstock.com, 9; © Blend Images/Shutterstock.com, 10; © George Clerk/iStockphoto, 11; © wavebreakmedia/Shutterstock.com, 13; © Praisaeng/Shutterstock.com, 14; © Lana Langlois/Shutterstock.com, 16; © JOAN FAIRMAN KANES/KRT/Newscom, 17; © Darios/Shutterstock.com, 18; © Photobac/Shutterstock.com, 19; © NASA, 20, 21, 22; © CREATISTA/Shutterstock.com, 24; © fstop123/iStockphoto, 25; © Yuri_Arcurs/iStockphoto, 26, 27; © Zippyzoo/iStockphoto, 28; © REUTERS/Alamy Stock Photo, 29

Graphic Element Credits: ©saki80/Shutterstock.com, back cover, front cover, multiple interior pages; ©queezz/Shutterstock.com, back cover, front cover, multiple interior pages; ©Ursa Major/Shutterstock.com, front cover, multiple interior pages; ©Zilu8/Shutterstock.com, multiple interior pages

45th Parallel Press is an imprint of Cherry Lake Publishing.

Library of Congress Cataloging-in-Publication Data has been filed and is available at catalog.loc.gov

Printed in the United States of America
Corporate Graphics

About the Author

Dr. Virginia Loh-Hagan is an author, university professor, former classroom teacher, and curriculum designer. She fails all the time. Each time, she fails better. (She loves Samuel Beckett's quote about failing.) She lives in San Diego with her very tall husband and very naughty dogs. To learn more about her, visit www.virginialoh.com.

Table of Contents

Introduction

People flop. They fail. Alexander Pope was a poet. He said, "To **err** is human." This means everyone make mistakes.

There are different types of mistakes. Some mistakes are good. They're smart. They teach people lessons. Mistakes are part of learning. They're part of science.

Some mistakes are bad. They're silly. People mess up their jobs. They make bad decisions. They make bad choices.

There are strange ways to fail. And then, there are **epic** fails. Epic means huge. These fails are super strange. They're so strange that they're hard to believe. They sound like fiction. But these stories are all true!

Mistakes can be painful.

chapter one

Building Fail

Architects design safe buildings. One architect failed. The John Hancock Tower is in Boston. It's the city's tallest building. The outside is made of windows. Windows let more light in. They give more city views.

In 1972, the glass panes started popping out. They crashed to the ground. This happened during high winds. Each window weighed 500 pounds (227 kilograms). All the windows had to be replaced.

The windows were designed badly. The windows had two layers. There was lead between the layers. Lead stretches

The tower also swayed too much. It needed more support.

when heated. It tightens when cooled. It changed too much. This stressed the glass. It caused the windows to break.

chapter two

Lottery Fail

A **lottery** is like a game. People buy tickets. They hope to win money. People pick numbers. Winners win by luck. Lottery winners claim their prizes. They show their winning tickets. One winner failed.

There's a woman in England. She plays the lottery every week. She writes the numbers down. She picked the winning numbers. But her husband trashed the ticket. She lost $181 million. It was the largest pot of money at that time.

She looked everywhere. She said, "He

Many people claim to lose lottery tickets.

loses everything I give him. … I was so angry at first. But there's no point in being angry about it."

chapter three

News Fail

News reporters write **obituaries**. Obituaries are death notices. Reporters write these reports about famous people. They do this before famous people die. They save the reports. They don't print them until the people actually die. But CNN failed to do this.

CNN stands for Cable News Network. CNN made a big mistake on April 16, 2003. It released obituaries of famous people. It reported President Ronald Reagan's death. It reported Nelson Mandela's death. It reported Pope John Paul II's death. There were many more.

Newspapers report the facts.

CNN blamed it on a computer problem. The problem was fixed. But people already saw it. Can you imagine reading your own obituary?!

chapter four

Surgery Fail

Surgeons are special doctors. They perform operations. They make people better. One failed.

Erica Parks is an Air Force officer. In 2010, she had a baby. She had an operation. Her surgeon left a **sponge** in her body. Sponges are thin squares. They're cotton bandages. They soak up blood.

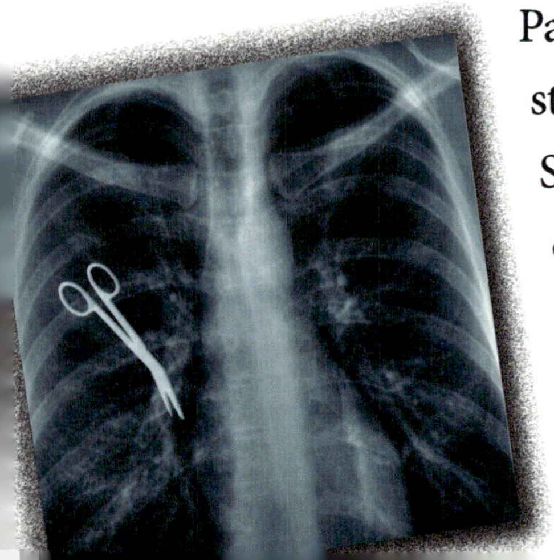

Parks was in pain for several weeks. Her stomach swelled up. Her gut shut down. She needed another operation. The operation lasted 6 hours. She stayed in

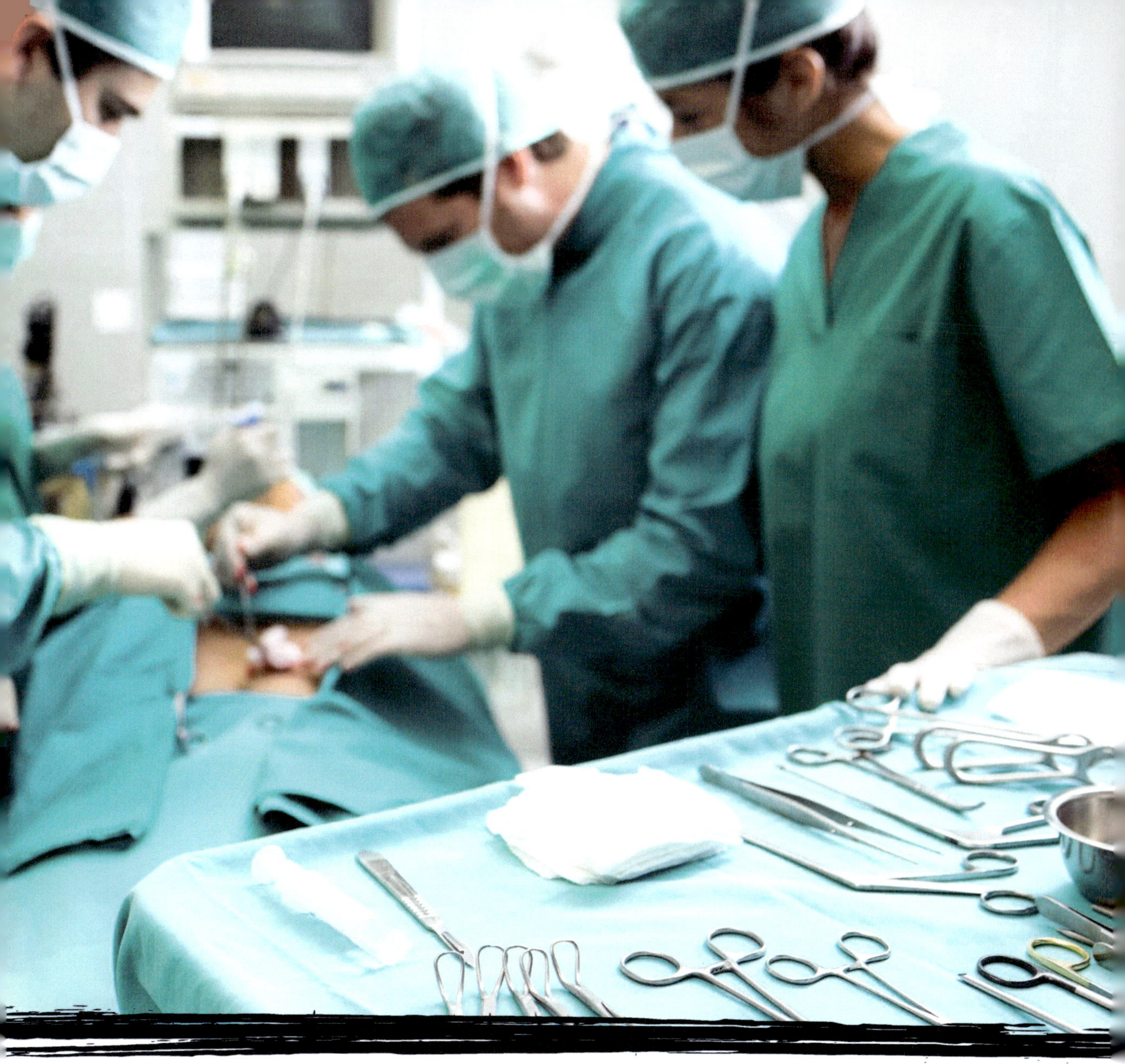

Items left in bodies cause infections.

the hospital for 3 weeks. This condition is called "**retained** surgical item." Retained means stuck. It happens about 12 times a day.

Another surgeon failed. This surgeon did the wrong operation. This is called "wrong **site** surgery." Site means place.

Fernando Ayala is from Mexico. He was blinded. He was 1 year old. He had cancer in his left eye. He got an operation. The surgeon took out the wrong eye. He took out Ayala's right eye. He said the right eye also had cancer. But the parents think that's a lie. The right eye was working well.

Ayala's mother said, "My baby does not have a working eye anymore. And nobody can put it back. It was his only healthy eye."

Surgery fails hurt people.

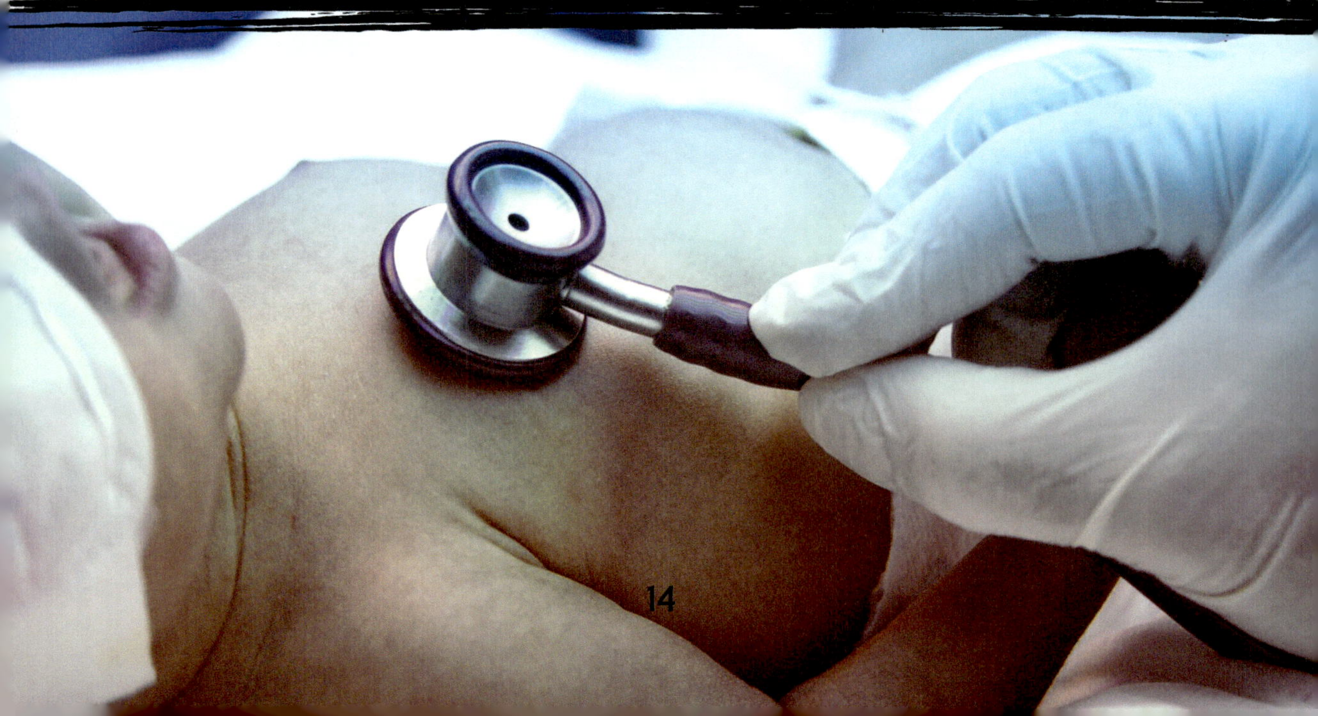

Explained by Science

Scientists study how human brains make decisions. Brains think about information. They think about sights. They think about sounds. They think about facts. They weigh everything. They make a decision. Brains have brain cells. These brain cells are called neurons. Neurons move. Scientists study this brain activity. Different parts of the brain make different decisions. Scientists studied people making mistakes. Mistakes cause movement in the front of the brain. It happens in the area behind the eyes. This area responds to the mistake. It helps people change behavior. Some people take drugs. That harms this brain area. Brain damage affects how people make decisions.

chapter five

Food Fail

Ketchup has one job. Its job is to make food taste better. It makes kids want to eat. It's red. Non-red ketchup failed.

This happened in 2000. Heinz is a company. It's famous for making ketchup. It invented Heinz EZ Squirt. It made ketchup in different colors. First, it made "Blastin' Green." There are green tomatoes. So, this made sense. It was a hit at first. Then, Heinz made other colors. They made purple, orange, pink, and blue ketchups.

Kids lost interest. Parents were grossed out. People mixed the colors together.

The green ketchup came out at the same time as the movie Shrek.

The ketchup became a yucky brown. It looked like watery poop. Nobody wanted to eat it.

chapter six

Rock Climbing Fail

Rock climbers climb rocks. They scale walls. One failed. Mitch Parker is a rock climber. He lived in a jungle in Belize. Belize is in Central America. He climbed a high cliff. He made a wrong move. He threw his rope into a hive. He was attacked by bees. He was stung over 1,000 times.

He said, "Within seconds they were covering my head, trying to get in my nose and my mouth." He dropped down past the hive. He jumped into a stream. He drowned the bees. He went to a hospital. Doctors counted over 150 stings behind one ear.

Rock climbing is dangerous even when you're not attacked by bees.

Chapter Seven

Space Fail

NASA is in charge of the U.S. space program. It builds space machines. In 1999, it failed.

NASA wanted to build a Mars **orbiter**. This is a space probe. It travels around Mars. It studies Mars. NASA hired an engineering company. The company built the orbiter. It used the English system of measurement. NASA used the metric system. These are two different systems. This caused mistakes. The **navigation** system was off. Navigation is the science of getting from place to place. The orbiter couldn't transfer information. So, it got lost in space. NASA

NASA stands for National Aeronautics and Space Administration.

lost $125 million. A NASA official said, “Everyone was amazed we didn’t catch it.”

NASA made another epic fail. Something historic happened on July 20, 1969. Humans landed on the moon. Neil Armstrong and Buzz Aldrin were **astronauts**. They're space scientists. They walked on the moon's surface. They were the first to do so.

It was filmed. But NASA lost the tapes. Richard Nafzger is a NASA engineer. He learned they were erased in the 1980s. The tapes were reused. This was to save money. NASA ran out of data storage tapes.

Nafzger said, "I think it slipped through the cracks. And nobody's happy about it."

NASA reported the missing tapes in 2006.

Spotlight Biography

Tony Ablewhite makes brain-training games. He works for Puzzler Media. He makes puzzles. He uses technology. He helps people make the most of their minds. He works with scientists and experts. He studies how people work puzzles. He studies how people make decisions. He studied 2,000 adults. He said, "We need to get better at making our own minds up." A person makes 773,618 decisions over a lifetime. He or she will regret 143,262 of them. An adult will make 27 decisions a day. The first decision is waking up. Each decision takes up to 9 minutes.

chapter eight

Parenting Fail

Parents take care of children. They're role models. One failed. Sandra Padilla Miranda is from Florida. Her daughter got in a fight at school. So Miranda set up a fight between her daughter and the other girl. The fight was at their apartment building. A large crowd watched. The girls started fighting. Someone recorded the fight.

Miranda encouraged the fight. She said, "Hit harder. Bite her." She was taken to jail. She was charged with child abuse. Miranda said she didn't want them fighting in school. She wanted to help them solve their problems.

The girls were ages 14 and 17.

chapter nine

Cop Fail

Cops help people. They solve crimes. One cop failed.

There was a hotel fire. It happened at the George Washington Hotel. It's in Pennsylvania. Firefighters found a strange room. They called the cops.

J. R. Blyth is a police chief. He's been a cop for over 35 years. He investigated the hotel room. Blood splattered the room. There was trash. There was a piece of **scalp**. Scalp is a human's head skin. Blyth described the room as the "most **grisly** murder scene." Grisly means scary. He

Some think the hotel is haunted.

spent over 8 hours investigating. Then, he found out the blood was fake. The room was a movie set.

chapter ten

World Record Fails

Some people have world records. Some do silly things. They fail to do heroic deeds. But they do interesting deeds.

Ilker Yilmaz is from Turkey. He has a record. He squirted milk the farthest. He did this from his eye. He squirted milk 9 feet and 2 inches (2.8 meters). He put milk in his hand. He snorted it. He held back his eyelid. Milk came out his left eye. Yilmaz has a special tear gland. Only a few people can do this.

He discovered his talent. He swam with friends. He saw water squirting from his eyes. He learned about the world record. He went for it.

Mike Moraal is from Canada. His record was 8.745 feet (2.7 m).

Kirby Roy is another epic fail. He has a strange record. He got the hardest kick in his **groin**. Groin means private parts.

Justice Smith is a fighter. He's very strong. He kicked Roy. He kicked him at 22 miles (35 kilometers) per hour. That's over 1,100 pounds (499 kg) of force. His kick lifted Roy off the floor.

Roy is really good at **karate**. Karate is a form of fighting. Roy can take punches. He can take kicks. He's used to it. He trained his body. He doesn't feel pain like others. Roy's bones are thicker and harder than others.

Roy's bones may be tough, but his organs can be injured.

Try This!

- Make a list of your failures. Have a friend make a list as well. Compare your lists. Talk about who failed more. Talk about who failed better. Talk about who failed worst.
- Do something that makes you struggle. Do something that is hard for you. Learn a new skill. Start a new hobby.
- Own your failure. Take responsibility. Don't blame others. Learn from your mistake.
- Make a list of decisions. Think about what you're going to do today. Think about the effects of your decisions. Every decision has consequences. Make good choices.
- Fix a mistake you made. It's never too late to right a wrong.

Consider This!

Take a Position! Reread the Table of Contents. Which story is the worst fail? Why is it the worst? Argue your point with reasons and evidence.

Say What? Some failures are good. Some failures are stupid. Describe each type. Include examples for each type. Explain the difference.

Think About It! Research how a mistake has led to an innovation. Innovations are useful inventions. They help people. They make life better. Think about one of your mistakes. How can you learn from your mistake?

Learn More!

- Boyer, Crispin. *Famous Fails! Mighty Mistakes, Mega Mishaps, & How a Mess Can Lead to Success!* Washington, DC: National Geographic Partners, 2016.
- Morse, Jenifer Corr. *Book of World Records 2016*. New York: Scholastic, 2015.
- Zuchora-Walske, Christine. *Your Head Shape Reveals Your Personality! Science's Biggest Mistakes about the Human Body*. Minneapolis: Lerner Publications, 2015.

Glossary

architects (AHR-kih-tekts) people who design buildings

astronauts (AS-truh-nawts) space scientists

epic (EP-ik) huge

err (AIR) to make a mistake, to make an error

grisly (GRIZ-lee) grim, morbid, scary

groin (GROIN) area including the hips and private parts

karate (kuh-RAH-tee) form of fighting developed in Japan

lottery (LAH-tur-ee) a game where people buy tickets and win money by chance

navigation (nav-ih-GAY-shuhn) the science of figuring out how to get from one place to another place

obituaries (oh-BIT-choo-air-eez) death notices

orbiter (OR-bit-ur) a space probe that travels around a planet

retained (rih-TAYND) kept, stuck

scalp (SKALP) skin of a human's head

site (SITE) place

sponge (SPUHNJ) bandage used in an operation to soak up blood

surgeons (SUR-juhnz) special doctors who perform operations

Index